YOUR PASSPORT TO

JAPAN

by Cheryl Kim

CAPSTONE PRESS
a capstone imprint

Published by Capstone Press, an imprint of Capstone
1710 Roe Crest Drive, North Mankato, Minnesota 56003
capstonepub.com

Library of Congress Cataloging-in-Publication Data
Names: Kim, Cheryl, author.
Title: Your passport to Japan / Cheryl Kim.
Description: North Mankato, Minnesota : Capstone Press, [2023] | Series:
World passport | Includes bibliographical references and index. |
Audience: Ages 8-11 | Audience: Grades 4-6 | Summary: "What is it like
to live in or visit Japan? What makes Japan's culture unique? Explore
the geography, traditions, and daily lives of the Japanese people"—
Provided by publisher.
Identifiers: LCCN 2022028967 (print) | LCCN 2022028968 (ebook) | ISBN
9781666390155 (hardcover) | ISBN 9781666390100 (paperback) | ISBN
9781666390117 (pdf) | ISBN 9781666390131 (Kindle edition)
Subjects: LCSH: Japan—Description and travel—Juvenile literature. |
Japan—Social life and customs—Juvenile literature.
Classification: LCC DS812 .K556 2023 (print) | LCC DS812 (ebook) | DDC
952—dc23/eng/20220622
LC record available at https://lccn.loc.gov/2022028967
LC ebook record available at https://lccn.loc.gov/2022028968

Editorial Credits
Editor: Carrie Sheely; Designer: Elyse White; Media Researcher: Morgan Walters;
Production Specialist: Tori Abraham

Image Credits
Alamy: Archivist, 10, CPA Media Pte Ltd, 9, World History Archive, 11; Capstone Press:
Eric Gohl, 5; Getty Images: David Finch, 29, DEA PICTURE LIBRARY, 8, DoctorEgg, 15,
Koji Watanabe, 18, 27, P A Thompson, 19, TOSHIFUMI KITAMURA/AFP, 25, urbancow, 21,
Yevhenii Dubinko, (stamps) design element; Shutterstock: Avigator Fortuner, 17, Dream28,
(flag) cover, Filip Bjorkman, (map silouhette) cover, Flipser, (passport pages) design
element , Fly_and_Dive, 12, MAHATHIR MOHD YASIN, 20, MicroOne, (stamps) design
element , pingebat, (stamps) design element , Sean Pavone, top middle 7, 16, sirtravelalot,
22, Travel mania, (bottom) cover, Win Jarusathit, bottom right 7

All internet sites appearing in back matter were available and accurate when this book was
sent to press.

CONTENTS

Words in **bold** are in the glossary.

CHAPTER ONE

WELCOME TO JAPAN!

The sun hits the top of a snowcapped **volcano**. The peak shimmers. Layers of rock, ash, and lava formed the majestic mountain. It stands 12,388 feet (3,776 meters) tall. Five peaceful lakes surround its base. This is Mt. Fuji, the tallest mountain in Japan. When the sun's rays sparkle at the top of the mountain, it is also known as Diamond Fuji. Mt. Fuji is an active volcano and one of Japan's most famous landmarks.

Japan is an island country in East Asia. It is made up of four main islands and a string of many smaller islands. The largest island is Honshu, followed by Hokkaido, Kyushu, and Shikoku. Japan is about the size of California. More than three times as many people live in Japan than California.

MAP OF JAPAN

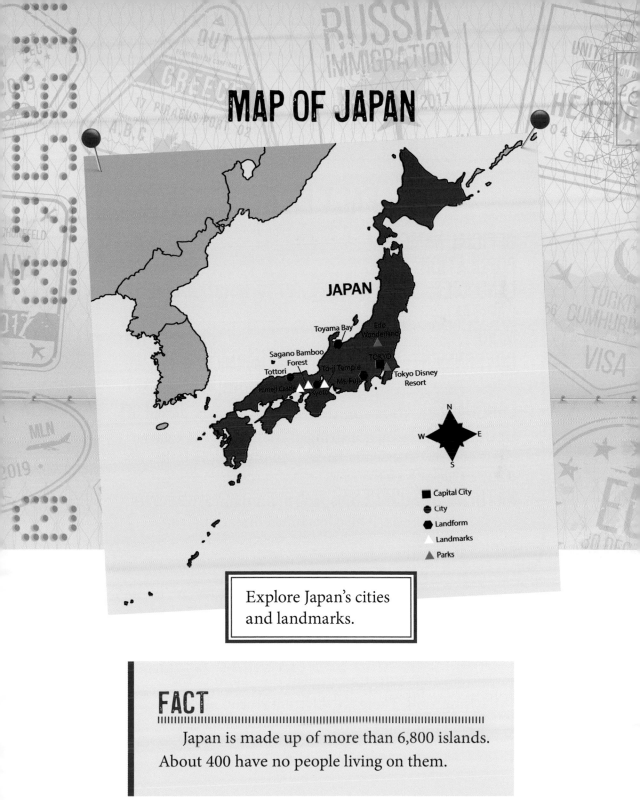

JAPAN

Toyama Bay

Edo
Wonderland

Sagano Bamboo
Forest

TOKYO

To-ji Temple

Tottori

Mt. Fuji

Tokyo Disney
Resort

Himeji Castle

Kyoto

N

W   E

S

■ Capital City

● City

⬡ Landform

△ Landmarks

▲ Parks

Explore Japan's cities
and landmarks.

FACT

Japan is made up of more than 6,800 islands.
About 400 have no people living on them.

FACT FILE

OFFICIAL NAME: ....JAPAN
POPULATION: 125,816,000
LAND AREA: ....145,937 SQ. MI. (377,976 SQ KM)
CAPITAL: ....TOKYO
MONEY: ....JAPANESE YEN
GOVERNMENT:...........CONSTITUTIONAL MONARCHY WITH TWO
LEGISLATIVE HOUSES
LANGUAGE: ....JAPANESE
GEOGRAPHY: Japan is a string of islands off the eastern coast of Asia. The Sea of Japan is to the west and the Pacific Ocean is to the east.
NATURAL RESOURCES: Japan's main natural resources are fish and forests. It also has limestone, coal, iron, gold, and silver.

FACT

Japan is sometimes called the "Land of the Rising Sun." There are different stories about where this name comes from.

Japan is home to 25 UNESCO World Heritage sites. These important places are protected. The country also has several large cities. The capital city of Japan is Tokyo. It is the largest city in the world by **population**.

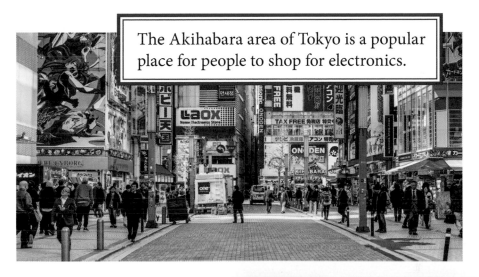

The Akihabara area of Tokyo is a popular place for people to shop for electronics.

Japan is a country that mixes old and new. It values its **traditions**. Yet Japan is also known for technology and for finding new ways to make products.

Itsukushima Shrine is one of Japan's World Heritage Sites. It was first built in the 500s and was rebuilt in the 1100s.

CHAPTER TWO

HISTORY OF JAPAN

Some of the first people to live in Japan were the Jōmon people. They lived in Japan more than 12,000 years ago. They survived by hunting animals and by gathering food such as berries and seeds.

Around 300 BCE, the Yayoi people came to Japan from China and Korea. They grew rice and made objects from metal. Separate **clans** controlled different areas. Later, some of these groups came together.

The Jōmon people lived in small communities near the sea or by rivers.

Empress Suiko

EMPRESS SUIKO

In the late 500s, Japan's first empress ruled. Empress Suiko was one of six children born to Emperor Kinmei. When her father and brothers died, she was asked to take the throne. The people thought she would make a great leader. After being asked three times, she agreed.

SHOGUNS AND SAMURAI

About 1,000 years ago, top military leaders called shoguns took control of Japan. They created armies with samurai soldiers. For more than 200 years, they closed off Japan to the rest of the world. Few people could leave or enter without approval. Western countries could not trade goods with Japan.

Samurai soldiers carried swords as their main weapon.

Over time, the power of the shoguns declined. Emperor Meiji became emperor in 1867. He wanted Japan to become modern. He began to make changes to Japan's government and **culture**. Farming and industries grew at a fast pace.

Emperor Meiji

WORLD AT WAR

Japan and the United States were on the same side during World War I (1914–1918). They fought with other countries against the Central powers. But during World War II (1939–1945), Japan and the United States fought on different sides. Japan bombed the U.S. navy base Pearl Harbor in 1941.

Four years later, the U.S. dropped atomic bombs on the Japanese cities of Hiroshima and Nagasaki. More than 150,000 people died, and many more became sick. After the war ended, Japan came under international control. In 1951, Japan became an independent nation again.

RECENT HISTORY

Different countries helped Japan rebuild. Japan became a leading **exporter** of cars and machinery. By the 1980s, Japan was one of the richest countries in the world.

In 2011, Japan was hit by an earthquake and tsunami. The earthquake was the largest one to hit Japan in recorded history. Since then, Japan has built some seawalls higher along its coasts.

The 2011 tsunami caused widespread damage to buildings in Japan's coastal areas.

TIMELINE OF JAPANESE HISTORY

ABOUT 32,000 BCE: The first people come to Japan.

10,000 BCE: The Jōmon people live in Japan for thousands of years.

300 BCE: The Yayoi people come to Honshu Island from Korea and China and begin farming rice and other products.

1100s CE: Military rulers known as shoguns take control of Japan.

1635: Japan closes to much of the outside world for more than 200 years.

1867: Emperor Meiji becomes ruler and brings changes to Japan's government and culture.

1914–1918: Japan fights in World War I alongside the Allies against the Central powers.

1941: Japan bombs Pearl Harbor during World War II.

1945: The U.S. drops atomic bombs on Hiroshima and Nagasaki.

1951: Forty-nine countries sign an agreement with Japan, returning Japan to an independent nation with full power.

1980: Japan becomes one of the world's most powerful economic countries.

2011: A damaging earthquake and tsunami hit Japan.

CHAPTER THREE
EXPLORE JAPAN

Four-fifths of Japan is covered in mountains. Many travelers visit Japan to see Mt. Fuji. Some stay at the base of the mountain to gaze upon its beauty. Others hike up the mountain in the summer. It takes about 5 to 10 hours to reach the top. Once there, visitors can send a postcard from Japan's highest post office. Visitors can also stamp their hiking sticks. Many watch the sunrise from the mountaintop.

Japan has many other natural wonders too. The Sagano Bamboo Forest of Arashiyama is one of the most photographed places in Japan. The swaying bamboo trees reach up to 65 feet (20 m) tall.

In Tottori, stunning sand dunes stretch to the sea for almost 10 miles (16 kilometers). In Toyama Bay, firefly squid light up the sea in a glowing blue.

People can enjoy the scenic areas around Mt. Fuji.

ANCIENT ARCHITECTURE

Pagodas, temples, and castles are spread out throughout Japan. Japan's pagodas are often five stories high. One of the most famous is the To-ji Temple pagoda in Kyoto. It was built in the early 800s and is a World Heritage site. Visitors also travel to Kyoto to see the many historic wooden townhouses called machiya. They are thousands of years old.

The five-story To-ji Temple is Japan's tallest wooden pagoda.

The buildings of the Himeji Castle grounds include a six-story main keep.

More than 100 castles are in Japan. Himeji Castle is one of the most famous. Built in the 1300s, it is one of Japan's national treasures.

TOKYO

Visitors from around the world travel to Tokyo. Cherry blossom trees line the streets. Tall towers light up the night sky.

Tokyo has unique areas. Harajuku is famous for its eye-catching fashion. Tokyo is known for its animal cafes. Diners can eat while petting cats, owls, bunnies, and hedgehogs.

Japan is home to more than 100 theme parks. Edo Wonderland is a history theme park recreating Japanese town life in the Edo period (1603–1867). At Sanrio Puroland, guests can meet Hello Kitty characters. At Universal Studios Japan, visitors can step into the first Super Nintendo World.

At Edo Wonderland, actors entertain visitors in shows.

Tokyo Disneyland is one of the busiest theme parks in the world.

The most popular theme park in Japan is the Tokyo Disney Resort. Tokyo Disney Sea is unique to Japan with water-themed attractions.

FACT

The Shibuya crossing in Tokyo is one of the world's busiest crosswalks. Up to 3,000 people cross at one time.

CHAPTER FOUR
DAILY LIFE

Over 98 percent of people living in Japan were born in the country. Chinese people and Koreans are two of the largest **minority** groups. The people of Japan are known for being polite and helpful. Many people live in city apartments. Some live in houses of traditional Japanese style called minkas.

Family life typically centers around work and school. Railways are one of the main ways workers and students get around. High-speed bullet trains connect Tokyo to other parts of the country.

Many of Japan's high-speed bullet trains can travel more than 200 miles (322 km) per hour.

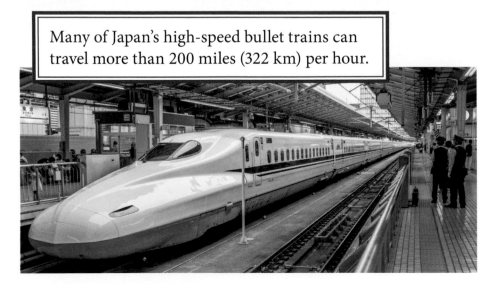

Most students in Japan wear uniforms to school.

FOOD

Traditional food is an important part of the Japanese culture. Meals are often made up of rice, miso soup, small side dishes, and Japanese pickles.

Sushi is one of the most well-known dishes. Sushi includes rice pressed with vinegar. The rice is often wrapped with raw seafood and vegetables.

A family enjoys a meal of sushi.

SUSHI

Sushi is the most famous Japanese dish outside of Japan. It is often served with soy sauce, wasabi, and pickled ginger.

Sushi Ingredients:
- 3 sheets of nori seaweed
- parchment paper
- 1 cup of Japanese short-grain rice (uncooked)
- 2 tablespoons rice wine vinegar
- 1 tablespoon sugar
- 2 cucumbers cut into long sticks

Sushi Directions:

1. Cook the sushi rice in a rice cooker or over the stove.
2. Microwave the rice wine vinegar and sugar for about 30 seconds.
3. Put the cooked rice in a large bowl. Add the rice wine vinegar mixture to the rice until it is fully coated and the rice has cooled.
4. Place one nori sheet shiny side down on a piece of parchment paper that is larger than the nori sheet by 3 inches (7.6 centimeters) on the top and bottom.
5. Pat handfuls of rice on top in a 1-cm thick layer, leaving the edges clear.
6. Add the cucumber strips on top of the rice.
7. Using the parchment paper, roll the sushi as tight as possible.
8. Cut each roll into individual sushi pieces.

Ramen is another popular Japanese dish. Wheat noodles are cooked in a fish or meat broth. Sliced pork or seaweed is often placed on top. It is flavored with miso or soy sauce.

CHAPTER FIVE
HOLIDAYS AND CELEBRATIONS

People in Japan celebrate several different holidays. Shōgatsu is the biggest celebration. It is the Japanese New Year. Many people visit shrines or temples.

During Golden Week, the nation celebrates four major holidays. One of those is Children's Day on May 5th. People go on picnics and to plays. Colorful kites and koinobori fish flags are flown. These carp fish are known for swimming upstream. They symbolize strength and success.

Japan has National Foundation Day on February 11th. The holiday celebrates the country's foundation and the first legendary emperor, Emperor Jimmu. A large parade is held in Tokyo.

People decorate streets for Shōgatsu each year.

Another patriotic holiday is the emperor's birthday. The Imperial Palace of Japan opens on this day to both locals and tourists. People wait for the imperial family to appear on the balcony. Many people wave the national flag.

CHAPTER SIX

SPORTS AND RECREATION

Baseball is the most watched and played sport in Japan. It came from the United States in the late 1800s. Baseball teams compete from the elementary level up to the professional leagues. The Japan National Baseball team won the International World Classic in 2006 and 2009. In 2021, Japan won the Olympic gold medal in baseball.

Another popular sport in Japan is sumo. It is a Japanese style of wrestling and the country's national sport. Weight gain is an important part of sumo training. The heavier the wrestler, the more force the opponent must use. Matches take place on a ring of clay and sand. The player who exits the ring or who first touches the ground with any body part except the feet loses. A contest can last from a few seconds to a few minutes.

Team Japan's baseball players celebrate winning the gold medal in 2021.

SHOHEI OHTANI

Major League Baseball (MLB) star Shohei Ohtani is a professional pitcher, hitter, and outfielder for the Los Angeles Angels. He grew up playing baseball at a young age in the small town of Oshu in northern Japan. He played Nippon Professional Baseball (NPB) before joining the MLB at the age of 23. He was **unanimously** voted the American League MVP in 2021.

ORIGAMI BOAT

In Japanese, *ori* means "to fold" and *kami* means "paper." The art of paper folding has been around in Japan since the Edo period. In the United States, it is called origami. Try making an origami boat.

1. Place a piece of paper in front of you with the shorter side on top. Fold the paper in half from top to bottom.
2. Fold in half again from left to right and reopen. Fold the top two corners together to the middle, forming a point, and crease.
3. Fold the top flap at the bottom of the paper up.
4. Turn over and fold the other bottom flap up.
5. Fold the end tabs in over each other so you have a triangle.
6. Place your thumbs into the opening at the bottom. Slowly pull apart the paper until it is flat again. Press along the folds.
7. At the top point, pull apart the two sides of folded paper until it makes a boat shape.
8. To float the boat in the water, tape around the bottom of the boat to keep the paper dry.

Judo is a Japanese martial art used for self-defense. It has roots in jiujitsu, which was originally created for the samurai. Most Japanese middle-school students learn judo or another martial art in school. Judo was added as an Olympic sport in 1964. Japan has won the most gold medals in judo.

Natsumi Tsunoda of Japan (right) competes at the Paris Judo Grand Slam in 2022.

A RICH CULTURE

Japan is a unique country. It has natural wonders, busy cities, and traditional arts and buildings. Japan's rich and colorful culture make it a special place to live and visit.

GLOSSARY

clan (KLAN)
a group of people who
are related

culture (KUHL-chuhr)
a people's way of life, ideas,
art, customs, and traditions

exporter (EK-sport-ur)
a sender of products to
another country to be sold

**minority
(mye-NOR-uh-tee)**
a group that makes
up a smaller part of a
larger group

**pagoda
(pah-GOH-dah)**
a shrine or temple shaped
like a tower with many roofs
that curve upward

**population
(pop-yuh-LAY-shuhn)**
the number of people living
in a place

**tradition
(truh-DISH-uhn)**
a custom, idea, or belief
passed down through time

**unanimously
(yoo-NAN-uh-muhss-lee)**
agreed on by everyone

volcano (vol-KAY-noh)
a mountain with vents
through which molten lava,
ash, and gas may erupt

READ MORE

Doeden, Matt. *Travel to Japan*. Minneapolis, MN: Lerner, 2022.

Harbo, Christopher. *10-Minute Origami Projects*. North Mankato, MN: Capstone, 2021.

Hoena, Blake. *Samurai: Japan's Noble Servant-Warriors*. North Mankato, MN: Capstone, 2019.

INTERNET SITES

Britannica Kids: Japan
kids.britannica.com/kids/article/Japan/345715

Kids Web Japan
web-japan.org/kidsweb/

National Geographic Kids: Japan
kids.nationalgeographic.com/geography/countries/article/japan

INDEX

ABOUT THE AUTHOR

Cheryl Kim is an elementary school teacher from California currently teaching at an international school in Thailand. When she's not teaching or writing, she enjoys travelling the world with her husband and sons.

SELECT BOOKS IN THIS SERIES

YOUR PASSPORT TO AUSTRALIA
YOUR PASSPORT TO BRAZIL
YOUR PASSPORT TO EGYPT
YOUR PASSPORT TO ENGLAND

YOUR PASSPORT TO GERMANY
YOUR PASSPORT TO JAPAN
YOUR PASSPORT TO MEXICO
YOUR PASSPORT TO SOUTH AFRICA